DISCOVER 🐾 DOGS WITH
THE AMERICAN CANINE ASSOCIATION

AMERICAN CANINE ASSOCIATION, INC.
ACA
America's Largest Veterinary
Health Tracking Canine
Registry
OFFICIAL SEAL ®

I LIKE

DALMATIANS!

Linda Bozzo

It is the Mission of the American Canine Association (ACA) to provide registered dog owners with the educational support needed for raising, training, showing, and breeding the healthiest pets expected by responsible pet owners throughout the world. Through our activities and services, we encourage and support the dog world in order to promote best-known husbandry standards as well as to ensure that the voice and needs of our customers are quickly and properly addressed.

Our continued support, commitment, and direction are guided by our customers, including veterinary, legal, and legislative advisors. ACA aims to provide the most efficient, cooperative, and courteous service to our customers and strives to set the standard for education and problem solving for all who depend on our services.

For more information, please visit www.acacanines.com, e-mail customerservice@acadogs.com, phone 1-800-651-8332, or write to the American Canine Association at PO Box 121107, Clermont, FL 34712.

Published in 2017 by Enslow Publishing, LLC.
101 W. 23rd Street, Suite 240, New York, NY 10011

Library of Congress Cataloging-in-Publication Data
Names: Bozzo, Linda.
Title: I like Dalmatians! / Linda Bozzo.
Description: New York, NY : Enslow Publishing, 2017. | Series: Discover dogs with the American Canine Association | Includes bibliographical references and index. | Audience: Ages 5 and up. | Audience: Grades K to 3.
Identifiers: LCCN 2016020284| ISBN 9780766081550 (library bound) | ISBN 9780766081536 (pbk.) | ISBN 9780766081543 (6-pack)
Subjects: LCSH: Dalmatian dog—Juvenile literature.
Classification: LCC SF429.D3 B69 2016 | DDC 636.72--dc23
LC record available at https://lccn.loc.gov/2016020284

Printed in China

To Our Readers: We have done our best to make sure all websites in this book were active and appropriate when we went to press. However, the author and the publisher have no control over and assume no liability for the material available on those websites or on any websites they may link to. Any comments or suggestions can be sent by e-mail to customerservice@enslow.com.

Photo Credits: Cover, p. 1 Rosa Jay/Shutterstock.com; p. 3 (left) Annette Kurka/Shutterstock.com; p. 3 (right) Aurelio Flrez/age fotostock/Getty Images; p. 5 Alena Ozerova/Shutterstock.com; p. 6. Bildagentur Zoonar GmbH/Shutterstock.com; p. 9 © iStockphoto.com/SolStock; pp. 10, 22 Rita Kochmarjova/Shutterstock.com; p. 13 (left) bikeriderlondon/Shutterstock.com; p 13 (right) © iStockphoto.com/jclegg (collar), Luisa Leal Photography/Shutterstock.com (bed), gvictoria/Shutterstock.com (brush), In-Finity/Shutterstock.com (dishes), © iStockphoto.com/Lisa Thornberg (leash, toys); p. 14 Photomorgana/Fuse/Getty Images; p. 15 Tannis Toohey/Toronto Star/Getty Images; p. 17 Richard Hutchings/Corbis Documentary/Getty Images; p. 18 Robert Daly/Caiaimage/Getty Images; p. 19 Katie-May Griffiths/Shutterstock.com; p. 21 Tina Rencelj/Shutterstock.com.

Enslow Publishing
101 W. 23rd Street
Suite 240
New York, NY 10011
USA
enslow.com

CONTENTS

IS A DALMATIAN RIGHT FOR YOU?

Dalmatians can make great family pets. They do best with active owners who spend lots of time at home.

Dalmatians are great for people who love to run!

A DOG OR A PUPPY?

Dalmatian puppies need kind, strong training. If you do not have time to train a puppy, an older Dalmatian may be better for your family.

Dalmatians grow to be medium to large in size.

Dalmatian puppies are born white. They get their spots in two or three weeks.

LOVING YOUR DALMATIAN

You can show your Dalmatian love by playing with him. Treat him with kindness.

EXERCISE

Dalmatians need lots of exercise. They are always ready for a long walk on a **leash**. Play games, like **fetch,** with your Dalmatian in a fenced-in yard.

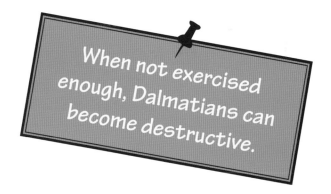

When not exercised enough, Dalmatians can become destructive.

FEEDING YOUR DALMATIAN

Dalmatians need a planned diet. Ask a **veterinarian (vet)**, a doctor for animals, which food is best for your dog and how much to feed her. Give your Dalmatian fresh, clean water every day.

Remember to keep your dog's food and water dishes clean. Dirty dishes can make a dog sick.

Do not feed your dog people food. It can make her sick.

Your new dog will need:

a collar with a tag

a bed

a brush

food and water dishes

a leash

toys

GROOMING

Dalmatians **shed** all the time. This means their hair fails out. Your Dalmatian should be brushed every day.

Use a gentle soap made just for dogs.

Your Dalmatian will need a bath every so often. A dog's nails need to be clipped. A vet or **groomer** can show you how. Your dog's ears should be cleaned, and her teeth should be brushed by an adult.

WHAT YOU SHOULD KNOW ABOUT DALMATIANS

Dalmatians can get into trouble if left alone for long periods of time. Dalmatians can have health issues, such as deafness.

Dalmatians can live up to 14 years.

Dalmatians are known as mascots for firehouses.

You will need to take your new dog to the vet for a checkup. He will need shots, called vaccinations, and yearly checkups to keep him healthy. If you think your dog may be sick or hurt, call your vet.

A GOOD FRIEND

Like a good friend, your Dalmatian will love to spend lots of time with you. Dalmatians get along with other family pets. They especially like horses.

NOTE TO PARENTS

It is important to consider having your dog spayed or neutered when the dog is young. Spaying and neutering are operations that prevent unwanted puppies and can help improve the overall health of your dog.

It is also a good idea to microchip your dog, in case he or she gets lost. A vet will implant a microchip under the skin containing an identification number that can be scanned at a vet's office or animal shelter. The microchip registry is contacted and the company uses the ID number to look up your information from a database.

Some towns require licenses for dogs, so be sure to check with your town clerk.

For more information, speak with a vet.

There are many dogs, young and old, waiting to be adopted from animal shelters and rescue groups.

fetch To go after a toy and bring it back.

groomer A person who bathes and brushes dogs.

leash A chain or strap that attaches to a dog's collar.

shed When dog hair falls out so new hair can grow.

vaccinations Shots that dogs need to stay healthy.

veterinarian (vet) A doctor for animals.

Books

Baines, Becky. *Everything Dogs*. Washington, DC: National Geographic Kids, 2012.

Brannon, Cecelia H. *All About Dogs*. New York, NY: Enslow Publishing, 2017.

Websites

American Canine Association Inc., Kids Corner
acakids.com
Visit the official website of the American Canine Association.

National Geographic for Kids, Pet Central
kids.nationalgeographic.com/explore/pet-central/
Learn more about dogs and other pets at the official site of the National Geographic Society for Kids.

INDEX